Cambridge Young Learners English Tests

Cambridge Movers 3

Examination papers from

University of Cambridge

ESOL Examinations:

English for Speakers of Other Languages

CAMBRIDGE UNIVERSITY PRESS

CAMBRIDGE UNIVERSITY PRESS
Cambridge, New York, Melbourne, Madrid, Cape Town, Singapore, São Paulo

Cambridge University Press
The Edinburgh Building, Cambridge CB2 2RU, UK

www.cambridge.org
Information on this title: www.cambridge.org/9780521755214

First published 2003
6th printing 2006

Printed in the United Kingdom at the University Press, Cambridge

A catalogue record for this publication is available from the British Library

ISBN-13 978-0-521-75521-4 Student's Book
ISBN-10 0-521-75521-2 Student's Book

ISBN-13 978-0-521-75522-1 Answer Booklet
ISBN-10 0-521-75522-0 Answer Booklet

ISBN-13 978-0-521-75523-8 Cassette
ISBN-10 0-521-75523-9 Cassette

<u>Contents</u>

Part 1
– 5 questions –

Listen and draw lines. There is one example.

Jim   Fred   Sally   Peter   Jill   Daisy   John

Part 2

– 5 questions –

Listen and write. There is one example.

	Name:	*Sue Clark*
1	How old:	
2	Lives in:	*Street.*
3	Library day:	
4	Number of books:	*a week.*
5	Kind of books:	*books about*

Part 3
– 5 questions –

What did John do last week?

Listen and write the correct day. There is one example.

> Monday, Tuesday, Wednesday, Thursday,
> Friday, Saturday, Sunday

Wednesday
....

....

Part 4
– 5 questions –

Listen and tick (✔) the box. There is one example.

What did Sam do at school today?

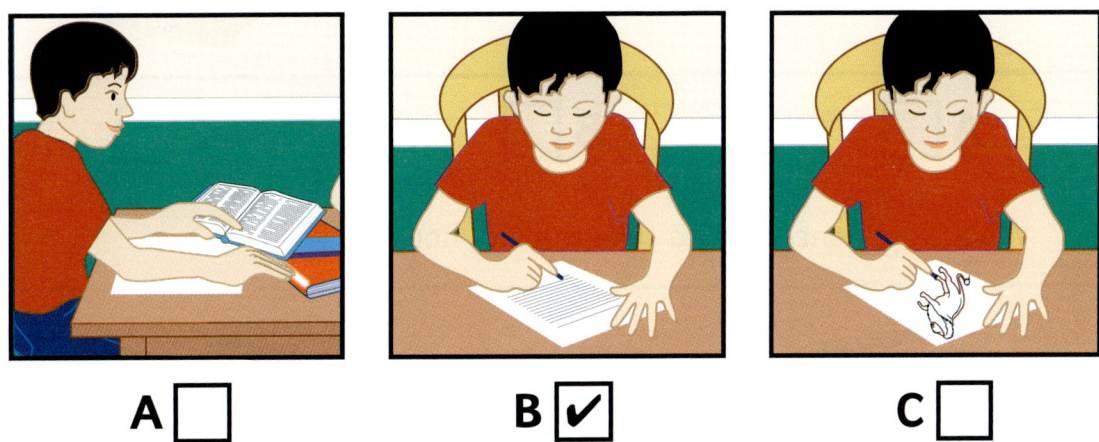

A ☐   B ✔   C ☐

1   What's the matter with Jill?

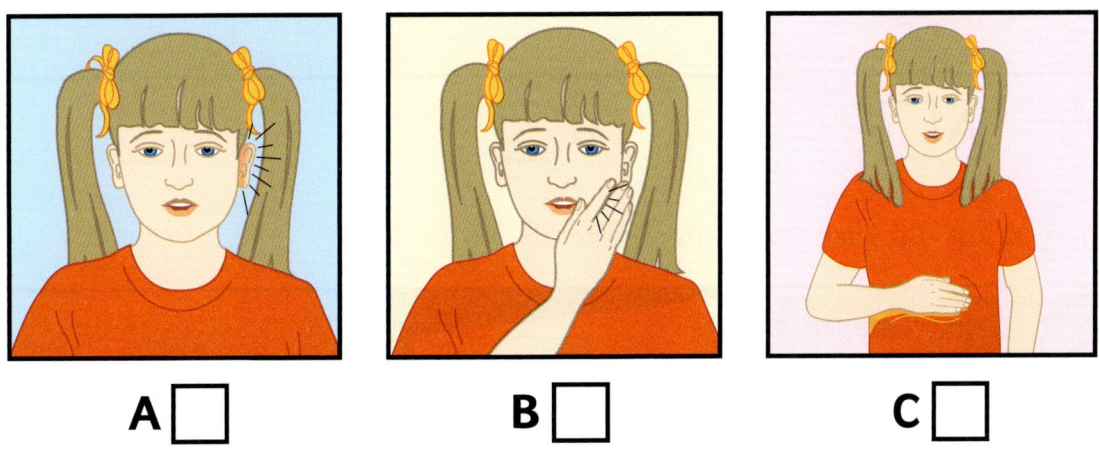

A ☐   B ☐   C ☐

2   Which child is Ben?

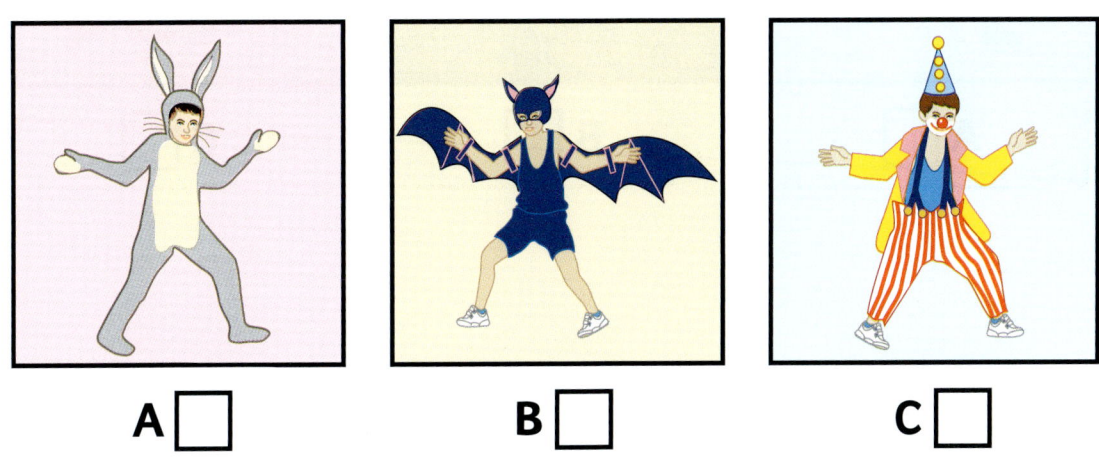

A ☐   B ☐   C ☐

3   What does John want for lunch?

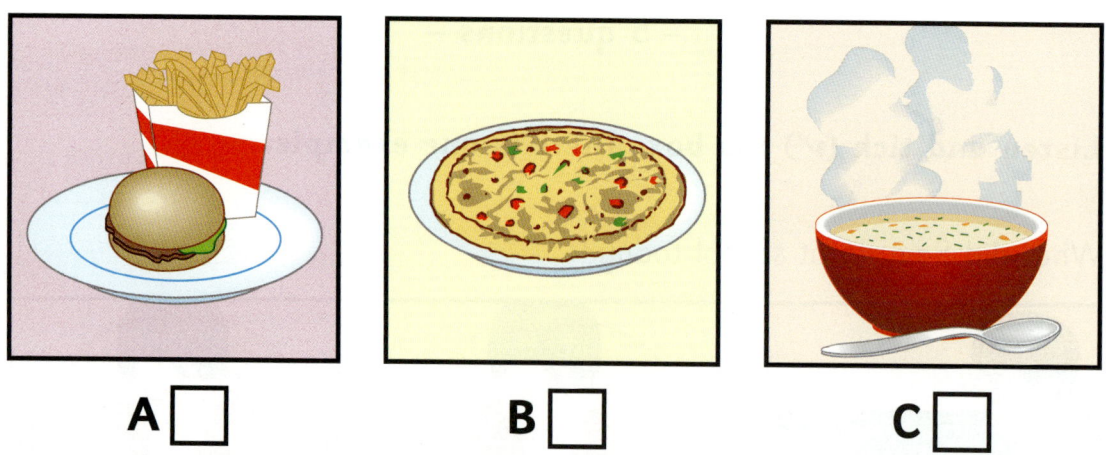

A ☐   B ☐   C ☐

4   What does Jane want to take to Jim's house?

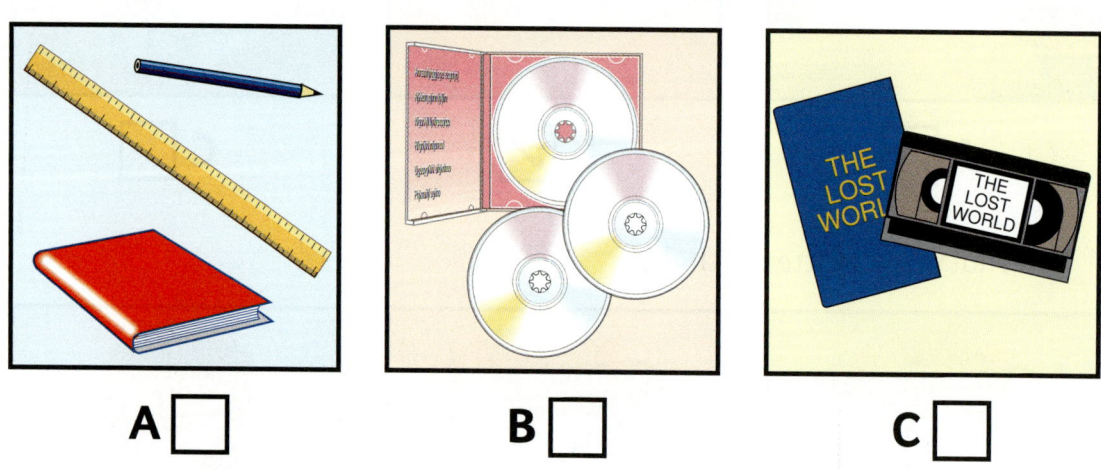

A ☐   B ☐   C ☐

5   What did Nick do at the weekend?

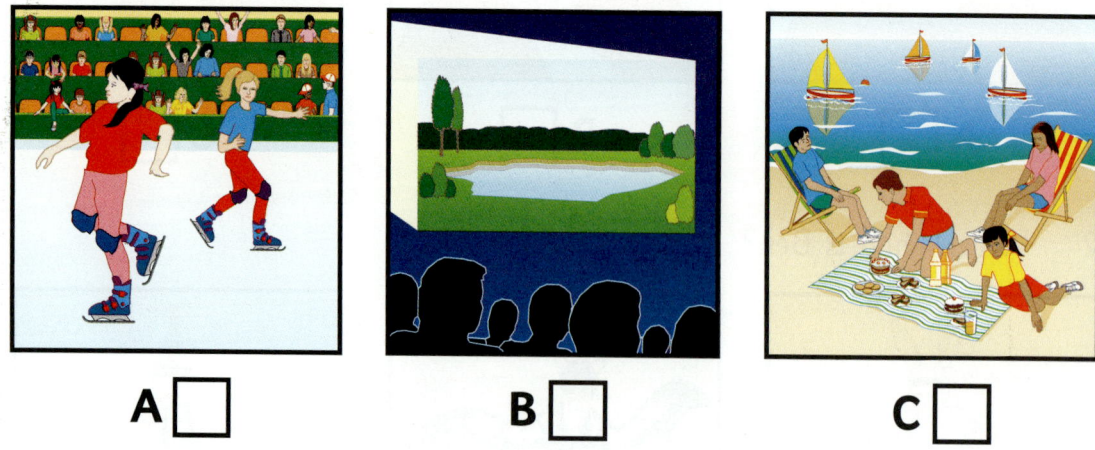

A ☐   B ☐   C ☐

Part 5
– 5 questions –

Listen and colour and draw. There is one example.

Reading and Writing

Part 1
– 6 questions –

Look and read. Choose the correct words and write them on the lines. There is one example.

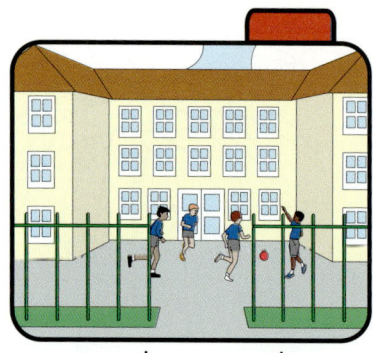

a playground

a clown

clouds

a market

a pirate

the sun

a farm

stars

Example

People can buy meat, fruit, clothes
and toys here. .... *a market* ....

Questions

1 People laugh at this person. He often has
   very big shoes, and paints his mouth red
   and his face white. ....

2 This is very hot. We see it in the day
   but not at night. ....

3 This is a person in stories who lives on
   a boat, sometimes finds treasure, and
   sometimes has a parrot. ....

4 These are white or grey. Rain comes
   from them. ....

5 Children run, shout and play games in
   this place, which is outside. ....

6 This place often has fields of fruit or
   vegetables and animals often live there. ....

Part 2
– 6 questions –

Look and read. Write yes or no.

Examples

All the children in the picture
are wearing hats.

.... *yes*

Two boys are swimming in
the water.

.... *no*

Questions

1   The tree has got snow on its leaves.   ....

2   The snowman is sitting under the
    umbrella.   ....

3   One of the children is having a shower.   ....

4   The house has a balcony above the door.   ....

5   The taller girl is drinking some orange
    juice.   ....

6   The shorter boy is wearing the longest
    scarf.   ....

Part 3
– 6 questions –

Read the text and choose the best answer.

Jane is asking her aunt about her holiday.

Example

Jane: Did you enjoy your holiday?

Aunt: A   Yes, please.

(B)   Yes, thank you.

C   Yes, OK.

Questions

1   Jane: Did you like the food?

Aunt: A   Most of it was good.

B   Yes, I was.

C   No, it didn't.

2   Jane: Did you understand the people?

    Aunt: A   Yes, I understand.

                B   Sometimes!

                C   No, they couldn't.

3   Jane: What did you see there?

    Aunt: A   Big parks, a zoo and some shops.

                B   At the cinema in the town.

                C   I see the beach every morning.

4   Jane: Were you afraid in the plane?

    Aunt: A   Only for the first five minutes.

                B   Because it was very loud.

                C   I watched the film.

5   Jane: What did you like best about the holiday?

    Aunt: A   The weather, because it was always sunny.

                B   My last holiday with your family.

                C   I'd like to see the different animals.

6   Jane: Are you happy to be home again?

    Aunt: A   Yes, it was a beautiful house.

                B   Yes, they were good to me.

                C   Yes, but I'd like to go there again one day.

Part 4
– 7 questions –

Read the story. Look at the pictures and the two examples.
Write one-word answers.

I go to the lake every Saturday because I love fishing. I often catch

a .... fish .... , and then my parents and I

.... eat .... it for supper. Last Saturday, I caught

nothing. Then I went home because it was wet and

.... all morning. I said, 'Hello' to my mum,

and put my fishing bag on the .... in the

kitchen. Then the bag started to move! 'Mum!' I said, 'What's in my

bag?' She .... and said, 'Well, I don't know!

It's your bag!'

She opened it and .... inside. Then she

shouted, 'Oh!' and a frog jumped out. We watched the frog, then I

caught it and put it in a big bowl of water and rocks. We were all

very hungry, and we had a big .... for

supper. Then Mum said, 'What about the frog? It's hungry. You must

catch some .... for it!'

What's the best name for this story?

Tick one box.

My family goes fishing ☐

I catch something different ☐

Supper by the lake ☐

Part 5
– 10 questions –

**Look at the pictures and read the story. Answer the questions.
Do not write more than three words.**

My name's Sally. Last Saturday, Bill, my favourite uncle, came to see us.
He had a big square box in his car. He picked it up carefully and carried it
to our garden. 'What's in the box?' we asked. He said, 'What do you think?'
My brother John said, 'Some toys,' and I said, 'A cake.' 'No,' Bill said, 'not
toys or cake.' We had lunch, and then Bill said, 'I'd like to go shopping!'

Example

When did Uncle Bill go to
see John and Sally?   last Saturday
....

Questions

1   Where did Bill put the box?   ....

2   What did Bill want to do after lunch?   ....

Bill bought a lot of things in the village that afternoon. He came out of the first shop with two round boxes. Then he went to a pet shop, and came out with a third box. It was bigger than the first two. Bill had to carry it. 'What's inside the boxes? Please tell us!' I said. 'Wait, Sally!' said Bill, and we went home.

3   Where were the shops that Bill went to?   ....

4   What kind of shop was the second shop?   ....

5   Who carried the biggest box?   ....

6   How many boxes did they take home?   ....

⇨

At home, Bill said, 'Open the boxes now.' First, Mum opened the square one. In it, there was a white duck! Then I opened the round boxes. There was one bowl for the duck's water, and one for its food. John opened the biggest box last. It was a house for the duck. 'Thank you, Bill! Now we can have eggs for breakfast every morning!' we said.

7   Where did they open the boxes?   ....

8   What was in the square box?   ....

9   Which boxes were the two bowls in?   ....

10 Who opened the last box?   ....

Blank Page ⇨

⇨

Part 6
– 5 questions –

Read the text. Choose the right words and write them on the lines.

JUNGLES

Jungles are hot, wet places. They are very green because on most

Example   days it ....rains.......... there. There are big rivers in most

1   jungles, and people often go .... boat because

2   that is easier .... walking. A lot of flowers, trees

3   and animals .... in jungles, and sometimes there

4   are villages. Some of the food .... we eat and

plants in our gardens come from jungles. They are only a small part

5   .... the world but they give us a lot.

Example	rain	raining	rains
1	in	by	on
2	than	like	and
3	living	live	lived
4	what	that	who
5	off	of	from

Part 1
– 5 questions –

Listen and draw lines. There is one example.

Paul   Nick   Sue   Peter   Jill   Ann   May

Part 2
– 5 questions –

Listen and write. There is one example.

	Name:	Jane Smart
1	How old:	....
2	Hair:	....
3	Favourite clothes:	....
4	Favourite hobby:	....
5	Pet:	....

Part 3
– 5 questions –

What did Bill do last week?

Listen and write the correct day. There is one example.

> Monday, Tuesday, Wednesday, Thursday,
> Friday, Saturday, Sunday

Monday

....

....

....

....

....

....

Part 4
– 5 questions –

Listen and tick (✔) the box. There is one example.

Where's Kim's comic?

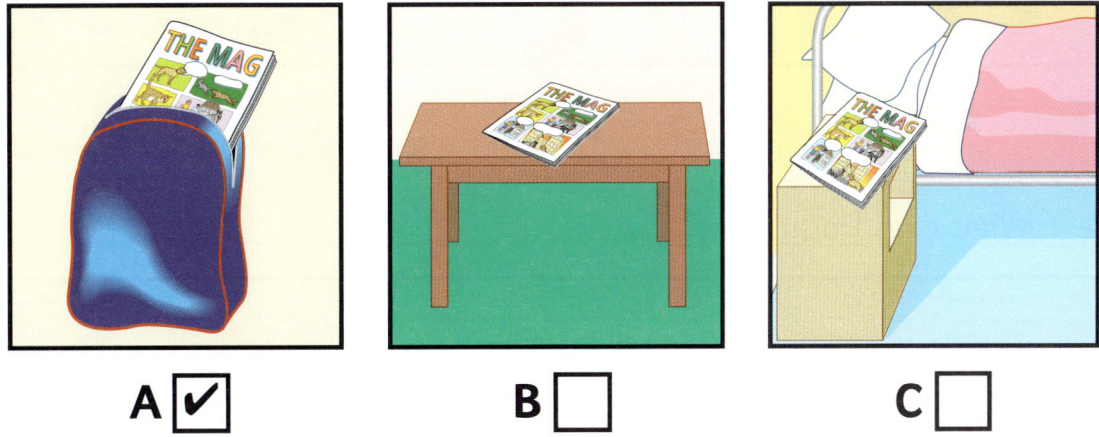

A ✔   B ☐   C ☐

1   Where does Sam's dad work?

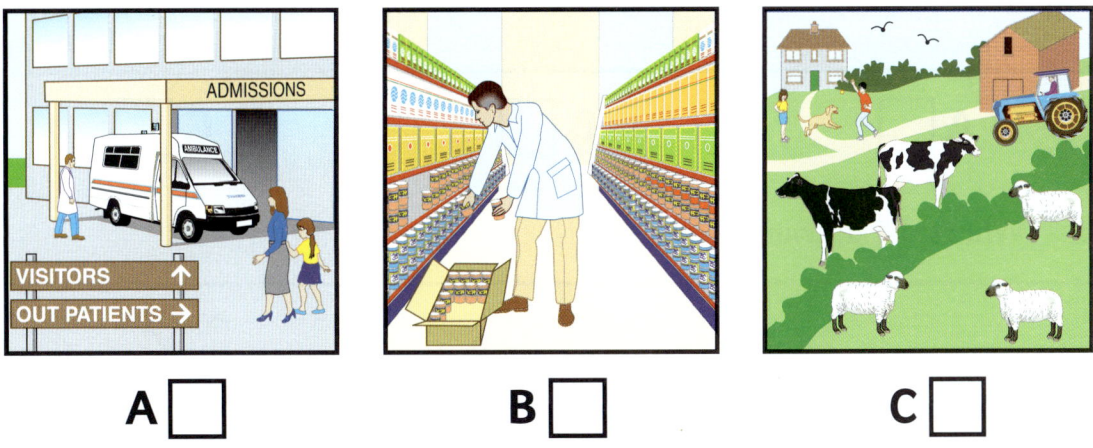

A ☐   B ☐   C ☐

2   What does Ann have to buy?

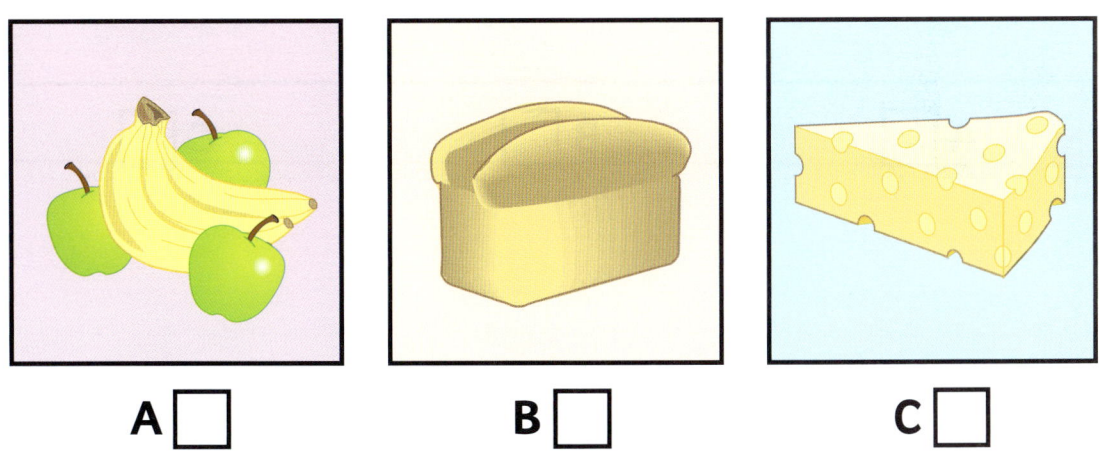

A ☐   B ☐   C ☐

3   Which is Jim's family?

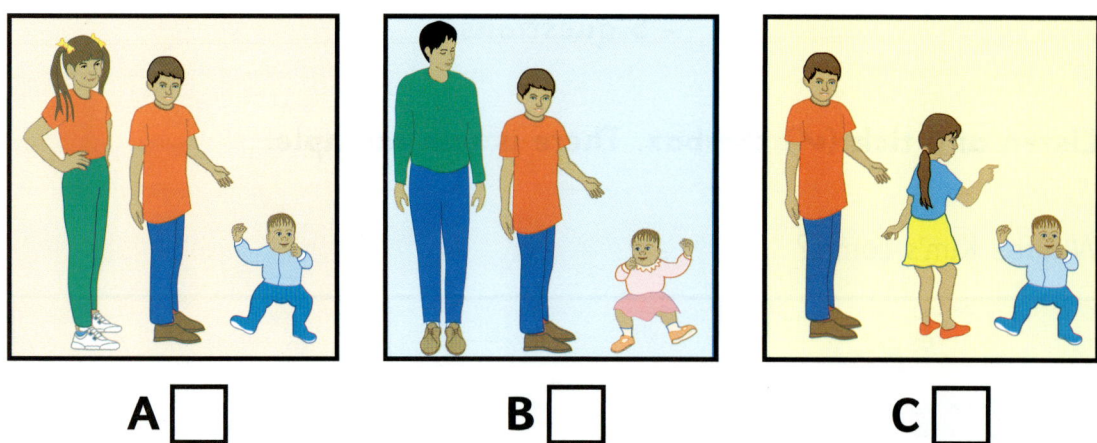

A   ☐   B   ☐   C   ☐

4   What does Daisy want?

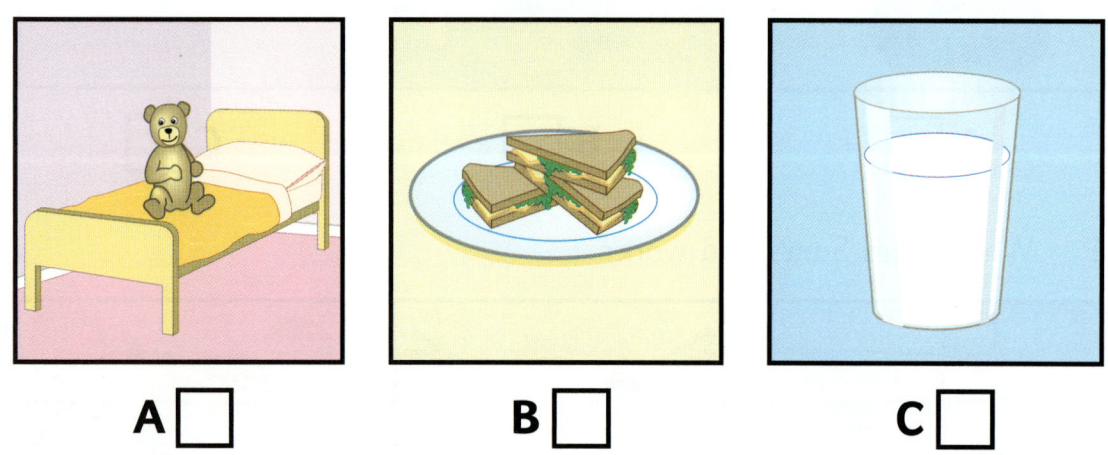

A   ☐   B   ☐   C   ☐

5   What's Jill drawing?

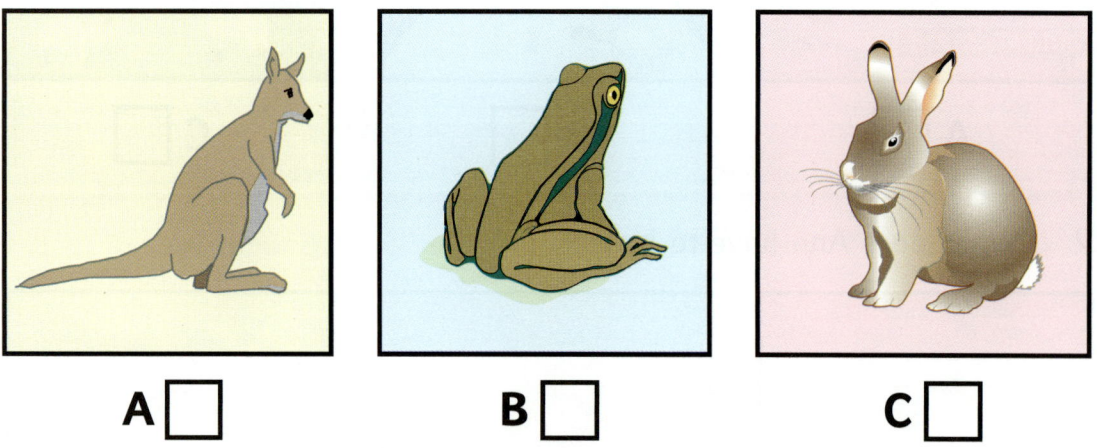

A   ☐   B   ☐   C   ☐

Part 5

– 5 questions –

Listen and colour and write. There is one example.

Part 1
– 6 questions –

Look and read. Choose the correct words and write them on the lines. There is one example.

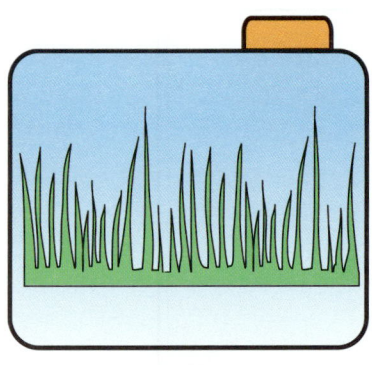

grass

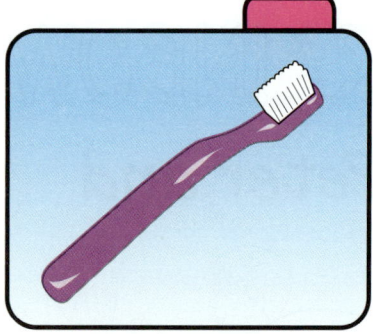

a toothbrush

a shower

trees

flowers

comics

videos

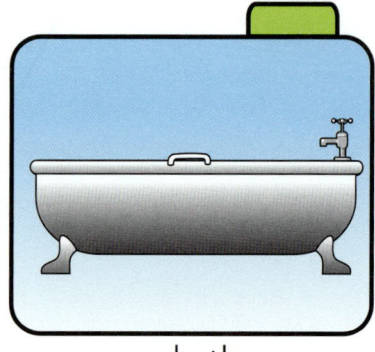

a bath

Example

This is green, and cows and
horses eat it.

..................*grass*..................

Questions

1   Most of these are green and brown.
They are sometimes very old and
they are often very tall.

....

2   These have got pages of pictures
and stories, and children enjoy
reading them.

....

3   You put hot and cold water in
this and then wash in it.

....

4   These plants are all colours and big
or small. People like having them in
their gardens and in their homes.

....

5   These are films that you can watch
at home.

....

6   You stand under this and water
comes out of it.

....

Part 2
– 6 questions –

Look and read. Write yes or no.

Examples

One person in the picture is talking
on a phone.   *yes*
....

The bus is in a city street.   *no*
....

Questions

1   The clown is sitting behind a boy who
    is reading.   ....

2   Most of the people on the bus are
    children.   ....

3   There is a woman with some fruit in
    her hand.   ....

4   All the people on the bus are wearing
    hats.   ....

5   The boy with the dog is wearing glasses.   ....

6   The tallest person on the bus is listening
    to music.   ....

Part 3
– 6 questions –

Read the text and choose the best answer.

Example

Paul: Good morning, Miss Young.

Miss Young: (A) Hello, Paul.
            B   Thank you, Paul.
            C   OK, Paul.

Questions

1   Paul: My brother Nick can't come to school today.

    Miss Young: A   Oh, is he coming now?
                 B   Oh, have you got any sisters?
                 C   Oh, why is that?

2   Paul: He's got a bad stomach-ache.

    Miss Young: A   It's hurting badly.

                  B   He's better, then.

                  C   Oh, I see.

3   Paul: Can we paint a picture to give to him?

    Miss Young: A   Yes, we can all paint one big one.

                  B   Yes, he paints very well.

                  C   Yes, we like painting him.

4   Paul: What can we paint?

    Miss Young: A   Paper and pens are on my table.

                  B   Well, he likes animals.

                  C   The picture he painted is the best.

5   Paul: He'd like a picture of the zoo. That's his favourite place.

    Miss Young: A   Yes, he enjoyed them.

                  B   OK, we can paint that, then.

                  C   Well, he likes his dog a lot.

6   Paul: And I can take it home for him this afternoon.

    Miss Young: A   All right, but be careful with it on the bus!

                  B   It's a beautiful picture.

                  C   He'd like that one.

Part 4
– 7 questions –

Read the story. Look at the pictures and the two examples.
Write one-word answers.

My mum and dad are very different. Mum has got straight, black

.................**hair**................. , but Dad's is ....**curly**................. .

Mum likes hot, ... weather, because she likes

being outside. Dad likes .... because he doesn't

like being hot. At weekends, Mum likes going to the lake, and she

.... there with me and my sister. Dad

.... on the lake in cold weather.

Our family has a lot of good holidays, because we go to the

.... in hot weather because Mum likes it, and

we go to the .... in cold weather because Dad

likes that!

What's the best name for this story?

Tick one box.

My favourite holiday   ☐

My mum and dad   ☐

Me and the weather   ☐

Part 5
– 10 questions –

Look at the pictures and read the story. Answer the questions.
Do not write more than three words.

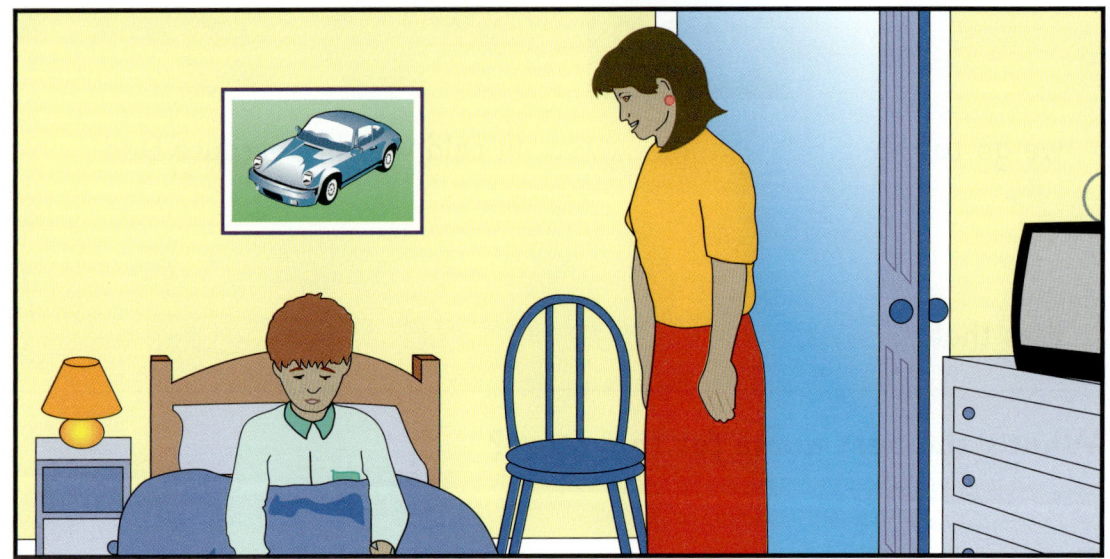

Last Monday, John came home from school with a headache. He didn't want to watch TV. He wanted to go to bed. But that night he didn't sleep very well, and in the morning he was tired and his head was hot. 'No school for you today!' his mum said. 'You can have breakfast in bed.' John wasn't very hungry, but he had some fruit and some orange juice. 'Now you must sleep,' his mum said.

Example

When did John come home
with a headache?   *last Monday*
....

Questions

1   What didn't John want to
     do after school?   ....

2   Where did he have breakfast?   ....

3   What did he drink?   ....

In the afternoon John woke up again, and went downstairs to the kitchen. His grandmother was there. 'Hello, John!' she said. 'Are you better now?' 'Yes, thank you,' John said. 'Where's Mum?' 'Your mum's at work,' his grandmother said. 'I'm having pasta for lunch. Would you like some?' 'Yes, please,' John said, and he ate a big bowl of pasta.

4   When did John wake up again?   ....

5   Who was in the kitchen?   ....

6   Where was John's mum?   ....

7   What did they eat for lunch?   ....

After lunch John had a shower, got dressed and took his favourite CDs from the cupboard. Then his mum phoned. 'Is John OK?' she asked. 'Is he sleeping?' 'Sleeping!' said his grandmother. 'No, he isn't. He's playing loud music in his bedroom. Now my head hurts!'

8   What did John take from the cupboard?   ....

9   Who phoned that afternoon?   ....

10   Where did John listen to music?   ....

Blank Page

Part 6

– 5 questions –

Read the text. Choose the right words and write them on the lines.

HELICOPTERS

Example Helicopters fly, but they ....*are*............. not like planes.

1 Most planes carry more people and are bigger ....

2 helicopters. Helicopters .... fly up and down,

and they sometimes go quickly and sometimes very slowly.

3 Helicopters are good for taking people .... and

from places which are difficult to go to quickly – mountains, for

example.

4 People .... need to go to hospital very quickly

5 sometimes go .... helicopters. In all parts

of the world, helicopters help a lot of people.

Example	are	do	did
1	or	than	but
2	would	shall	can
3	to	of	at
4	who	which	what
5	in	on	by

Listening

Part 1
– 5 questions –

Listen and draw lines. There is one example.

Jane   Fred   Daisy   Jill   Jim   John   Sally

Part 2
– 5 questions –

Listen and write. There is one example.

The Children's Zoo

Name: Ann .... *Jones* ....

1   Lives at: .... Field Road

2   Time: Sunday ....

3   Animals: ....

4   Working with: Mr ....

5   Phone number: ....

Part 3
– 5 questions –

What did Paul do last week?

Listen and write the correct day. There is one example.

> Monday, Tuesday, Wednesday, Thursday,
> Friday, Saturday, Sunday

Monday
....

....

....

....

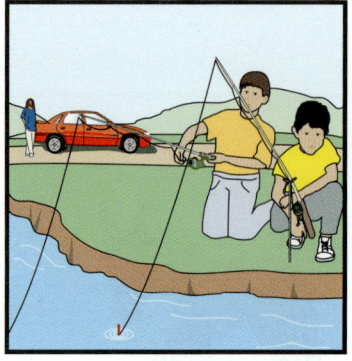

....

....

Part 4

– 5 questions –

Listen and tick (✔) the box. There is one example.

What did Fred do at school today?

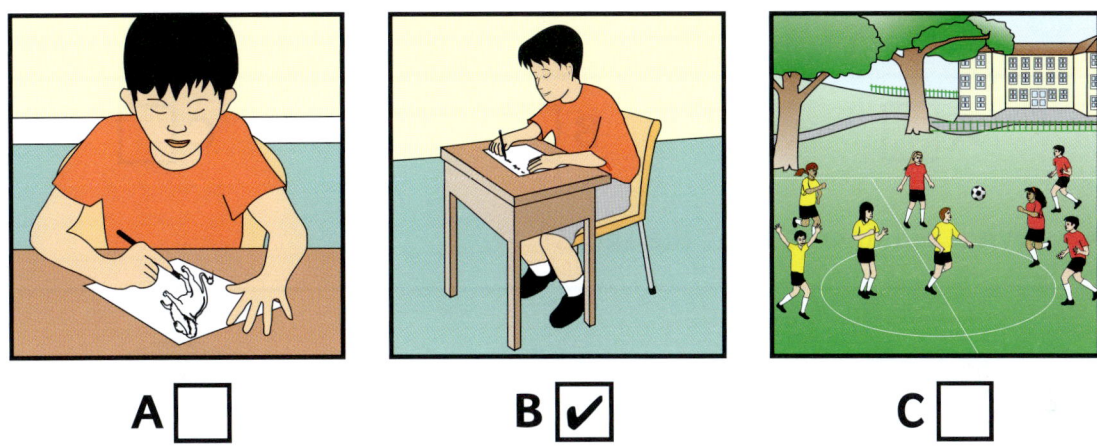

A ☐　　　　B ✔　　　　C ☐

1　What's Sue doing?

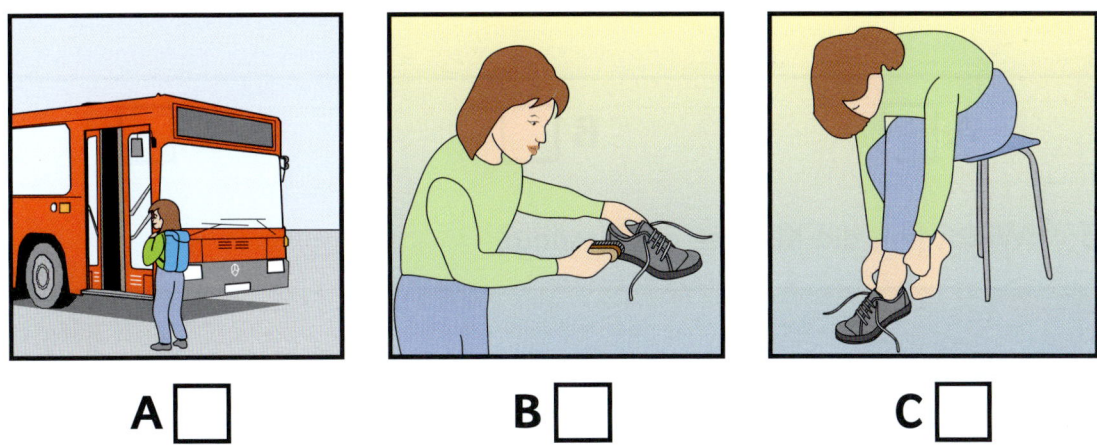

A ☐　　　　B ☐　　　　C ☐

2　What's for supper?

A ☐　　　　B ☐　　　　C ☐

3   Which toothbrush is Ben's?

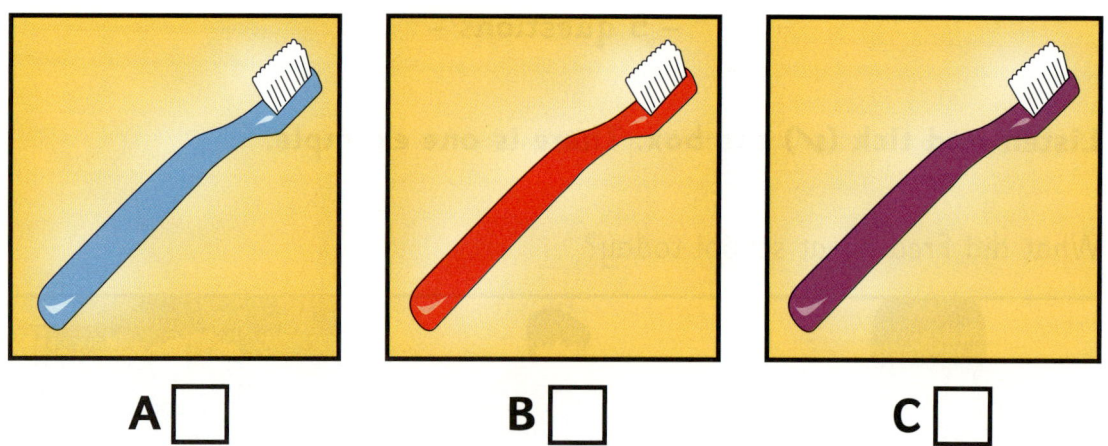

A ☐   B ☐   C ☐

4   What did John buy at the shops?

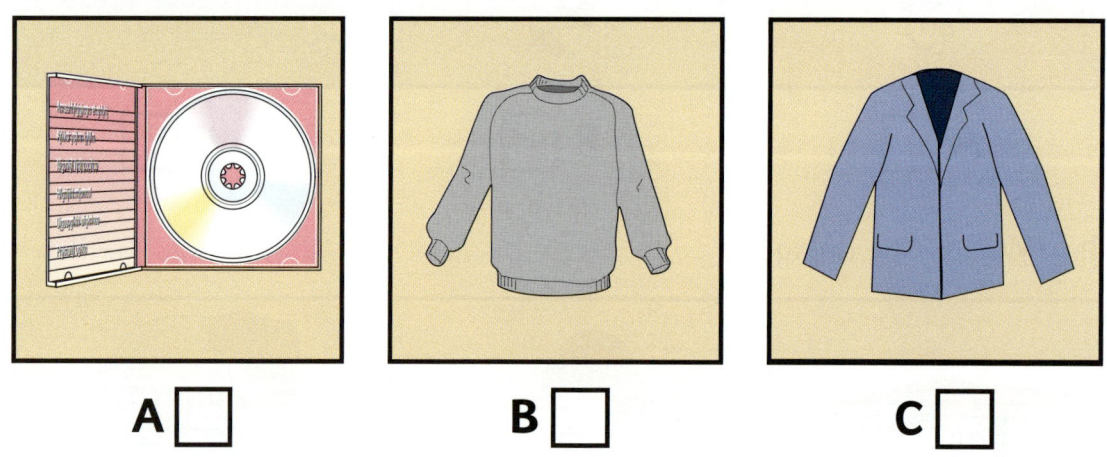

A ☐   B ☐   C ☐

5   Which film did Kim see on Tuesday?

A ☐   B ☐   C ☐

Part 5
– 5 questions –

Listen and colour and draw. There is one example.

Part 1
– 6 questions –

Look and read. Choose the correct words and write them on the lines. There is one example.

Example

You can listen to people talking or playing
music on this, but you can't see them.   ....*a radio*...............

Questions

1   You find people, houses and shops in this
     place. It is smaller than a city or town.   ....

2   You walk up or down these. They
     take you from one floor of the house
     to another floor.   ....

3   We can see this in the day. It's very,
     very hot.   ....

4   People cook in this room and they
     sometimes eat there.   ....

5   You sit down at this and play
     music on it.   ....

6   Some animals live in these. You find
     them in the country and they often
     have grass in them.   ....

Part 2
– 6 questions –

Look and read. Write yes or no.

Examples

The baby is sitting on the grass and
playing with a black and white sock.   *yes*
....

The older woman is giving the younger
woman a towel.   *no*
....

Questions

1   One of the girls has a fish on her sweater.   ....

2   There's a blue shirt on the grass.   ....

3   The cat is running up the tree next
     to the house.   ....

4   The girl on the chair is reading a comic.   ....

5   One of the windows is round.   ....

6   Most of the clothes in this picture are red.   ....

Part 3
– 6 questions –

Read the text and choose the best answer.

Example

Jim: Hello, Ann. What book are you reading?

Ann: A   A famous person.

           Ⓑ One about famous people.

           C   One for famous people.

Questions

1   Jim: Do you like reading about famous people?

    Ann: A   Yes, I do.

            B   Yes, I am.

            C   Yes, I have.

2   Jim: What did the woman in that photo do?

     Ann: A   She'd like to go climbing.

               B   She must climb mountains.

               C   She climbed the biggest mountain in the world.

3   Jim: Was she the first woman to do it?

     Ann: A   Yes, she was.

               B   Yes, she does.

               C   Yes, she did.

4   Jim: Who did she climb with?

     Ann: A   Six of her friends.

               B   With a bag on her back.

               C   Very slowly and carefully.

5   Jim: When did she start climbing mountains?

     Ann: A   Every morning.

               B   At sixteen.

               C   Because she enjoys it.

6   Jim: Can I read that book now, please?

     Ann: A   Sorry, my mum wants it after me.

               B   Here they are.

               C   Yes, you can read.

Part 4
– 7 questions –

Read the story. Look at the pictures and the two examples. Write one-word answers.

Last Saturday Mary and Nick .... *rode* .... to the forest

with their .... *dog* .... , Pat. They took Pat's favourite ball

with them. They sat down by the .... in the forest

and watched the ducks, but the ducks were afraid of Pat. Mary

.... the ball for Pat, but it went behind some trees.

Pat ran there, but he didn't come out! Then they saw him with

something in his mouth. It was a woman's ....!

Mary and Nick took it and .... inside. They found the woman's name and phone number. At home they phoned her

and then went to her house. She gave them some ....

and tea and Pat had a .... of meat.

What's the best name for this story?

Tick one box.

Mary's dog doesn't come home ☐

Pat finds something in the forest ☐

Dogs don't like ducks ☐

Part 5
– 10 questions –

**Look at the pictures and read the story. Answer the questions.
Do not write more than three words.**

Last Sunday Bill and his brother Nick went to the beach. First they played tennis, and then Nick said, 'I'm hot. Do you want to go swimming now?' Bill said, 'Yes,' and they took off their clothes and put them on the rocks.

Example

When did Bill and Nick go to
the beach?   .... last Sunday ......

Questions

1   What game did the boys play at
    the beach?   ....

2   Why did Nick want to
    go swimming?   because ....

3   Where did they put their clothes?   ....

Bill and Nick took the ball to the sea, because they wanted to play with it in the water. But it was difficult, because they couldn't stand up very well. Then they tried to find sea animals at the bottom of the sea and Nick pointed at something in front of him. Bill picked it up and they swam to the rocks again. 'Look! It's your T-shirt!' Bill shouted. They looked on the rocks, but their clothes weren't there and they could see their towels in the water!

4   What did they try to play with
     in the sea?   ....

5   What did they want to find
     in the sea?   ....

6   Who picked up the T-shirt?   ....

7   Where were their towels?   ....

They found all their things in the sea and put on their wet shirts and trousers. They went to wait for the bus, but it didn't come very quickly and they went to phone their mum. She came in the car to take them home. They were very cold and at home their mum gave them some hot tea.

8   What clothes did the boys put on?   ....

9   Who did the boys go home with?   ....

10   What did the boys drink at home?   ....

Blank Page ⇨

Part 6
– 5 questions –

Read the text. Choose the right words and write them on the lines.

COMPUTERS

Example	When we first had computers, they were ....*very*............................ big
	and they only added numbers. One computer was bigger
1	.... a small bedroom! Now computers can do a
2	lot more things and .... are some which you can
	carry in a bag or pick up in one hand! You can find computers in
3	schools, ... work and in the home. Often you
	want to go on the computer in the evening and you
4	.... to wait for your brother, sister, mum or dad
	to stop working, playing games, or writing to a friend in
5	.... place.

Example	well	very	more
1	but	or	than
2	there	their	they
3	at	in	on
4	can	must	have
5	one	another	different

Blank Page

Speaking

Find the difference

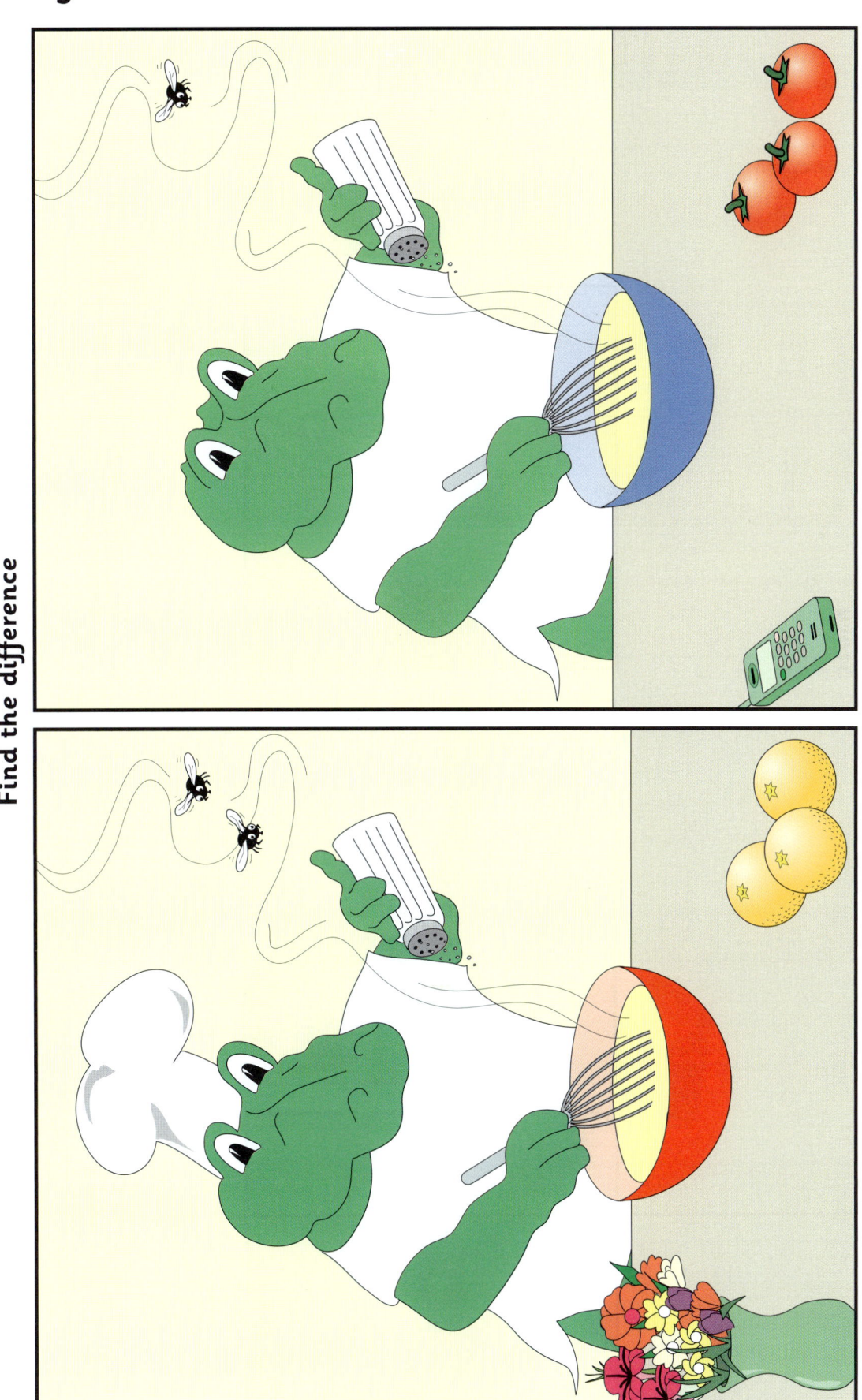

Story

Find the different ones

Blank Page

Test 2
Speaking

Find the difference

Story

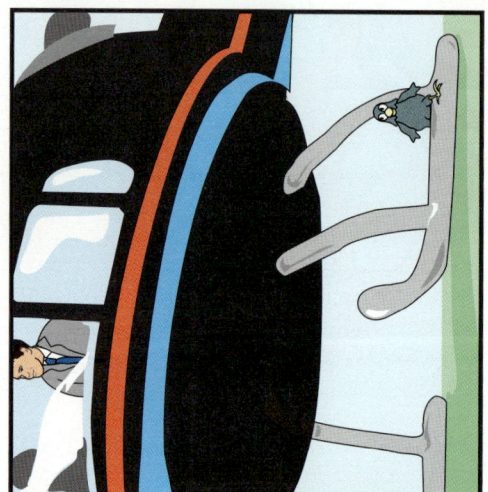

Find the different ones

Blank Page

Find the difference

Story

Find the different ones